CORNISH HURLING

A Study In The Popular Survival
Of Magical Ritual

R.D. Greenaway

OAKMAGIC PUBLICATIONS

CORNISH HURLING

A Study In the Popular Survival
Of Magical Ritual

R.D. Greenaway

First published by the author in 1926

This edition:
OAKMAGIC PUBLICATIONS 2004

ISBN: 1 904330 62 2

OAKMAGIC PUBLICATIONS,
PO BOX 67,
MONMOUTH NP25 3YP.

For a list of over 100 titles on Cornish
legends and folklore, send SAE to the
publisher at the above address.

www.oakmagicpublications.com

Tel: 07714110460

CORNISH HURLING

A STUDY IN THE POPULAR SURVIVAL OF MAGICAL RITUAL.

By R. D. Greenaway, A.I.S.A.

The following paper is virtually an expansion of a short note contributed to the correspondence columns of the " Western Morning News " at the beginning of the present year.* The conclusions there presented being to some extent new, and a further examination of the evidence giving me no cause to alter the main argument, I have endeavoured to set out here both evidence and conclusions at length. In the Cornish game known as Hurling, as played in the great hurling matches, its rules are few and simple. The players are divided into two parties, not necessarily equal in numbers. Each " side " has its own " goal," the goals being usually a considerable distance, sometimes two miles or more, apart. The ball, of wood covered with silver, is thrown up at a point roughly equidistant between the goals and it is then the endeavour of each side to convey it to its own goal. The actual play approximates to a faction fight with the ball as the bone of contention. The side which first got the ball to its own

---

* " Western Morning News," February 25th, 1925.

goal was counted the winning one, and when this was done the game was over. The ball as a rule became the property of the individual player who had succeeded (to borrow a term from a better-known game) in "touching-down" for his side. It was as a rule very highly prized by its possessor, and often kept " in the family " as a species of heirloom. (It may be remarked that the silver coating is probably a refinement added at some remote time to give additional value to the prize.) *

The antiquity of the game in this form is unquestionable. The earliest writers on the subject of Cornish popular customs speak of it as commonly played and have no suggestion to make as to the manner or date of its origin. At the same time, by the end of the 18th or beginning of the 19th century it was also played by country people at other times of the year, apart from the great hurling matches. This form of the game differed somewhat from the other ; there was a specified number of players on each side, the silver ball was dispensed with (stones or even turnips were often used) and a very elaborate code of rules was enforced. This modification of the game does not appear to have been known to Carew, who describes the simpler form at some length, and the existence of the aforesaid code of rules, lacking in the great hurling matches, is a clear indication of the development of the more complex form from the simpler one ; for a study of those games which have undergone a process of development in time shows always a change from simpler forms with a minimum of rule and complication to more complex and formal types ; a process which may be studied in games so dissimilar as football, chess and the various card games including and based on whist. That a game of this character can have undergone a reverse evolution, starting as a complex game with elaborate rules is *prima facie* unlikely ; and Carew's descrip-

---

* The classical description is in Carew, " Survey of Cornwall," 74.

2

tion of the game seems to make it clear that the complex form was unknown in his time. This form then may be regarded as developing out of the simpler one, which was played only on one occasion in the year (that is, played " in form," for practice bouts were always held before the great occasion). It is to this older form that we must, therefore, confine ourselves in considering the origin of the game.

As just stated, the great hurling matches took place once a year, the match day being nearly always in February. Thus at St. Columb the correct day was Shrove Tuesday; at St. Ives, the Monday immediately following Quinquagesima Sunday. At Helston it was held unusually late—on the 2nd May. But in general the match took place in February.*

The division of sides varied. At one time the games seem often to have been between the people of two adjoining parishes; but such contests seem to have become extinct about a century ago. At St. Ives the division was between men of the given names of William, John, and Thomas and " the Rest." At St. Columb the townsfolk competed against the country people. At Truro the married men were opposed to the bachelors, and so on.†

Such is, or was, the game of hurling. Now the comparative study of custom shows that this game is not peculiarly Cornish; on the contrary, it has a wide distribution in Great Britain. To the evidence for this statement I must now pass.

In the town of Derby, down to quite recent times, the parishioners of All Saints' and St. Peter's contended each Shrove Tuesday in a " football " match. A very large ball of leather stuffed with shavings was used. It might be

---

* Cf. Courtney, " Cornish Feasts and Folklore," 20.
† Courtney, loc cit.

either carried or kicked. Each side had its goal, these being on opposite sides of the town ; and the ball being thrown up in the market place it was the task of either side to get it to its own goal. The player who actually " goaled " the ball was chaired through the town to the accompaniment of merry peals on the bells of the winning parish's church.*

The correspondence of the above with the hurling game is too obvious to need emphasis. In one detail only it differs—the nature and size of the ball; but we shall see later that this difference is not of importance. It is a typical example ; and in the enumeration of other examples which follows I will, to save time, omit description, merely noting any special features.

Games similar to that at Derby were held at Ashborne (also in Derbyshire) ; Alnwick (Northumberland) ; Dorking ; Epsom ; Twickenham ; Kingston ; Teddington ; Bromfield (Cumberland) ; Chester (until 1539, when the disorders attendant upon it caused its suppression by the city authorities, footraces being substituted) ; in a large number of Scottish towns and villages, particularly in Scone, Melrose, Jedburgh, and Kirkwall; and in parts of Wales, notably in Cardiganshire and Pembrokeshire. The games held at Llanwenog in the former county and Pwlldu in the latter were especially popular.† Finally we find the custom outside this country altogether—namely in Brittany, where

---

* Journ. Arch. Assoc. (1852), vii, 203.

† Brand, " Popular Antiqq., i. 92 (Alnwick) ; Journ. A.A., loc. cit (Ashborne) ; Lysons, " Magna Britt," (ed. 1810), ii, 585 (Chester) ; Hutchinson, " Hist. of Cumberland," ii, 322 (Bromfield) ; " Book of Days," i, 214 (Jedburgh) ; Sinclair " Stat. Acc. of Scotland " (1796), xviii, 88 (Scone) ; ibid., xvi, 19 (Inverness in Midlothian) ; Wade " Hist. of Melrose Abbey," 144 (Melrose) ; " Times " newspaper, 7th March, 1862 (Dorking) ; " N. and Q.," 3rd series, i, 439 (Epsom) ; Hone " Everyday Book," i, 245 (Twickenham, Teddington, Kingston) ; Gomme, " Village Community," 242 (authorities not cited) (Kirkwall) ; ibid., 243 (quoting " Oswestry Observer " newspaper of 2nd March, 1887) (Cardinganshire) ; Dyer, " British Popular Customs," 88 (quoting Kennett MS.) (Flintshire) ; ibid., loc. cit, quoting Mason (Tenby) ; Fenton, " Tour through Pembrokeshire," 495 (Pwlldu).

4

it appears to have been widely spread among the peasantry in a form closely resembling the Cornish one, called " La Soule," a name the real meaning of which is unknown.*

The geographical distribution of these ball-games is of interest. As we have seen, they occur throughout England, Wales, and Scotland, and are particularly well developed in those parts of Great Britain which are ethnically Keltic. A Keltic origin seems certain ; and since the game seems to be unknown in Ireland it would appear to have some claim to be regarded as peculiarly British. Its existence in Brittany is most simply accounted for by the theory that it was imported into that district during the 5th century of the present era, at which period a great exodus to Armorica of Britons, and particularly of the inhabitants of southern and south-western Britain, took place.

In all the above cases the parallel to the Derby " football " match and to the hurling game is exact so far as essential features are concerned. The ball was usually a leather one stuffed with straw or some soft material, and of fair size. The Llanwenog ball was a bladder covered with pigskin and called the " pig." The Pwlldu ball was interesting as approaching the Cornish one—it was of wood, about the size of a cricket ball, boiled in tallow to make it slippery. These differences are not significant as regards the essential identity of the game. The ball remained the property of the winning side and particularly of the player who had " goaled " it. The Scone game had an interesting provision, not paralleled elsewhere, by which, in the event of neither side winning, the ball was cut in half at sunset and half given to each side. Throughout we find that as in Cornwall success in the game was counted a great honour both to the winning side and the individual player.

---

* Cf. Rio, " Petite Chouannerie " (I give this reference from memory, not having the work by me, and cannot give exact page.)

The division of sides varied in different parts but the game was very frequently inter-parochial. In the Scottish lowlands other systems of division were frequently met with, e.g., east v. west, or married v. bachelors. At Bromfield two parties apparently taken at random from within the village competed.

Finally, the time at which the game took place corresponds in general with the times of the Cornish hurling matches. In all the English cases,* and many of the Scottish ones, the match was held on Shrove Tuesday. But in Scotland at some places it was held a little earlier, on Candlemas Day (2nd February).

I have, I hope, made it clear that the hurling game is not peculiarly Cornish. It is true that elsewhere the game is spoken of as " football "; but as I have shown the method of play is the same. It must be remembered that football was originally played almost exactly as it is in these special " football " games, but with, if anything, a less regard to any rule. It was in fact a simple ball game in which the ball was of a size and consistency to permit of its being kicked. In its early days it was frowned upon as a recreation of idlers and vagabonds, and enactments were even passed against it. The small hard ball of the Cornish game, is as we have seen, paralleled in Wales.

One point about all these games is very striking. It is the fact that they are all held only once a year and always within a certain fairly well-defined period—between the end of winter and the early part of spring, while most of them are held in February. Now it is a useful principle in the investigation of popular customs that periodicity in a custom gives ground for a suspicion that it may have its origin in a ritual act—I mean by " ritual " that of magic or religion.

* With the exception of the game at Pwlldu, which took place on the 1st April.

An 'old' hurling ball (note the band and rivets) and a 'new' ball (made by a modern bonding process and showing the traditional inscription)

The reason is simple; it lies in the close connection of primitive thought and magico-religious action with the periodicity of natural processes. Now, the hurling game and the " football " games just discussed are periodic; are they, then, the survivals of something more than a mere game? At first the idea may seem doubtful, even a little ludicrous; but let us see what light anthropology throws on the subject.

The practice of magic, for ends personal or collective, is universal throughout mankind. In point of time, it goes back at least as far as the latter part of the Old Stone Age. The essential feature of magic lies in the endeavour of the magician to compel certain results by the performance of a ritual act. Magical practice takes many forms; but we are now concerned with only one of these.

One of the most impressive things to all savages (with the exception, to some extent, of those living in tropical forests) is the succession of the seasons. There are two main reasons. In the first place, the events are striking in themselves. In Continental Europe, for example, the death and decay of nature in winter and its triumphant resurrection in spring could not fail to impress the stupidest savage; and savages as a whole are far from stupid. In the second place, primitive man has more utilitarian reasons for concern about the matter. It must be remembered that he lives very much in the present; he is never *sure* that the death of nature in winter would always be followed by resurrection in spring. Perhaps one year it might die altogether, with disastrous results. Besides, a bad summer meant short commons, even to a hunter; and when, in his slow and painful progress, he became from a hunter an agriculturist, the question of the annual revival of nature in general and the vegetable world in particular had for him an interest paramount above everything, for a " bad year " might mean annihilation for him and his kinsfolk. So throughout the world we find him doing what he can, by means magical or religious or both, to avert this haunting danger. To the savage, there is little if any real gulf between things animate and inanimate; in fact, to him, often, all is animate or at least has the potentiality of animation. Feeling thus, it is not so difficult to see how he felt himself able by his own actions to control the course of nature. And his emotional outlook towards this question of nature's death and revival found its outlet, by a simple psychological process, in imitative ritual. The life of summer died—to rise again? To him, it *must* rise again; and so he ensured its doing so by an actual drama, or rather what a Greek would have called a *dromenon*, a " thing done " in which its death and revival were represented. But this was not the only way in which the matter might present itself to him. The shift of the seasons was interpretable as a combat between winter and summer, or between darkness and death on the one hand and light and life on the other. So often we find him dramatizing this too, by a mimic battle between the actors representing these two opposing principles.*

I must now give some examples. Most of these exist as survivals in popular custom in Europe, where for climatic reasons this type of imitative magic bit deep into primitive life. In many of the savage races of to-day the preculiarities of tropical climates have not been favourable to the development of a ritual of this type; and in Australia,

---

* For a general review of magical practice, consult Frazer " Golden Bough," *passim.* (In all cases when reference is made to the " Golden Bough " [" G.B."] the numbers of pages and chapters refer, unless otherwise stated, to the edition in one volume published in 1922, as being most easily accessible.) Cf. also two valuable short studies in Haddon, " Magic and Fetichism " (first part) and Harrison, " Ancient Art and Ritual " (first four chapters). For the evidence as to Old Stone Age magic, consult Burkitt, " Prehistory " (2nd ed.), the chapters on Cave Art, and particularly chap. 22. This gives references to other literature on the subject (see Bibliography therein).

one of the last strongholds of really " primitive " man, his attention was paid more directly to the food supply.* The Drama of Death and Resurrection I omit for the time as not to our purpose, confining myself to what may be called the " Battle of Summer and Winter."

In Bavaria, down to the 'fifties, every village had its " battle " on the fourth Sunday in Lent, between a man dressed as Summer in green garments and carrying a bough, and one representing Winter, and dressed in furs and carrying a snow-shovel. After a procession through the village, a combat ensued in which Winter was beaten by Summer and driven out of the village or ducked in a pond.† In Sweden there was a sham fight between the party of Winter and that of Summer ; the leader of the former dressed in furs and that of the latter covered with leaves and flowers ; this took place on May-day.‡ At Goepfritz in Austria the ceremony took place on Shrove Tuesday ; the representatives of Winter and Summer did not fight but sang verses against each other.§ At Dromling in Brunswick a man takes the part of Winter and after a tussle is driven out of the village by the young men and girls—this at Whitsuntide.|| In the Murom district of Russia, at the ceremony called the " Funeral of Kostroma " at the end of June, a mock combat took place over the " corpse " of Kostroma (a puppet of straw) ; in which, however, the party of Winter was victorious.¶ In the Isle of Man, the May-day games included a fight between the parties of Spring and Winter.** Finally, I will give two examples, with a wide geographical separation, one of which, I think,

---

* For this subject, consult Frazer, " Totemism and Exogamy," i, chap. I-IV, and references there cited.
† " G.B.," 316.
‡ Ibid., loc. cit.
§ Ibid., 317.
|| Ibid., loc. cit.
¶ Ibid., 318.
** Train, " Hist. of the Isle of Man," ii, 118.

The Hon. T.C. Agar—Robartes of
Lanhydrock throwing—up the silver
ball on Shrove Tuesday, 1911.

explains the other. Among the central Eskimo tribes, a tug-of-war is held at the *beginning of winter* between " Ptarmigans " and " Ducks " ; if the former win, the winter will be severe ; if the latter, it will be a favourable one.* This is an actual magical practice and not merely a survival ; and it is of special interest, because there was an exactly similar practice, except as regards date, at Ludlow in Shropshire. Every Shrove Tuesday there was a tug-of-war between two parties, each recruited from two of the wards. The rope was provided by the Corporation. The common belief was that this custom had its origin in an event in the Wars of the Roses ; but it is clearly a survival from far earlier times.† A similar custom is recorded from the North-west Provinces of India.‡

The examples given above might be added to, but they are, I think, sufficient for the purpose. The differences in the time at which the ceremonies are held are for the most part not of particular importance. In the Russian example, it must be remembered that although the " technique " is that of the other cases, the ceremony has the intention of representing the death of *Summer* and not of Winter ; while in the Eskimo example it is not difficult to see that in an Arctic climate the actors are far more concerned about the conditions in winter than those of summer. For the rest, they fall in much the same period as the ball-games—between the beginning of February and the middle of May. One case, we have seen, falls exactly on Shrove Tuesday. Further, we may turn to a kindred custom—that of " Killing the Carnival," widespread in Europe. Here a grotesque figure, after being carried in procession, is solemnly burnt or buried. This always takes place on Shrove Tuesday or Ash Wednesday. Frazer has

---

* " G.B.," 317.
† Dyer, work cited, 85 (citing " Hist. and Antiq. of Ludlow ").
‡ " Folklore Record," Vol. V, p. 36.

shown how the " Carnival " is actually the embodiment in effigy of the spirit of vegetation, which dies in winter but to live again in spring.* And it is not difficult to see how such a ceremony in agricultural Europe comes to take place so early in the year, when the lengthening days give the first promise of spring and the thoughts of the farmer are turned to the sowing of the crops.

Let us now see what progress we have made in our examination of the ball-games. We have examined them and found three elements which appear in all of them. They are :—

(i) Periodical celebration, nearly always just before or just after the beginning of spring.

(ii) The feature of the combat between opposing sides.

(iii) The ball as the centre of this combat.

Leaving (iii) out of consideration for a moment we turn to the " Battle of Summer and Winter " and find again features (i) and (ii). The resemblance can hardly be fortuitous ; and we seem led to the conclusion that in the ball-games we have a variant of the ritual acts described as performed to ensure the rebirth of summer.

There remains, however, a serious difficulty. The third element is not found in these instances of the " Battle of Summer and Winter " which we have examined. Now this element is an important one and we must find some explanation of its presence, otherwise our theory stands on an unstable basis.

One view that occurred to me in first studying the subject was that it was a merely fortuitous introduction. The ball as a toy has been known from remote times and

---

* Cf. " G.B.," chap. xxviii, *passim.* It is interesting to note that in the Carnival at Lerida (Catalonia) a mimic battle took place over the effigy, just as at the " Funeral of Kostroma."

has always been popular in these islands. The " Battle of Summer and Winter " would naturally lend itself to transformation into a ball-game, once its original meaning had been forgotten and it had become a mere survival. Thus the ball may have been introduced as a means of adding interest and excitement to a custom which was in itself becoming tedious. But this view, though plausible, will not stand close examination. If we adopt it, we have to explain why the " Battle of Summer and Winter " has survived in its ordinary form outside of this country, among peoples to whom also the ball is well known, and ball-games of various kinds common. Further, it does not adequately explain why such value is set on the ball itself— so that it usually becomes a cherished possession of the successful player, and in Cornwall at any rate was often handed down as an heirloom. At St. Ives (if my information is correct) it was looked upon as bringing good luck.* For these reasons I think this explanation must be set aside.

Now it seems on the face of it likely that some light might be thrown on the subject if we could find any game or rite in which the ball-game found a parallel, but in which the object of contention was not a ball, but something else. Fortunately, there is reliable record of at least two such cases; still more fortunately, they are both English, so that they may be used with the more confidence for comparative purposes.

The first of these customs hails from the Isle of Axhey in Lincolnshire. It was celebrated on Twelfth Day, and was a close copy of the ball-games, the difference being (i) that instead of a ball the disputed object was a *hood*, or according to another account a roll of canvas called a " hood." (ii) That the people from all the neighbouring villages took part, each set of villagers trying to get the

---

* Letter from Mr. Morton Nance, " Western Morning News," February 27th, 1925.

St. Columb

Shrove Tuesday 1951 — a comparatively
small number of hurlers hurling the ball
down Fore Street at a great pace

15

hood to their own village, there being no division into two sides. (iii) That certain men called " boggons " were deputed to endeavour to prevent this by keeping the hood within the boundaries of the field within which it was thrown up. The hood might be either thrown or kicked.*

The other case is even more significant. At Brough in Westmorland, also on Twelfth Day (or rather Twelfth Night) a holly-tree with lighted torches tied to it was carried in procession round the streets, and afterwards placed in the middle of the village and contended for by the villagers, who divided themselves into two parties, each attempting to drag it to their own goal (in this case a public-house).†

The resemblance of these customs to the ball-games is clear. It is true that they take place earlier in the year ; but I do not think that this presents any serious difficulty. But they are of extreme significance in another way. At Brough we have a *tree* as the object of dispute. Now all over Europe we find, in the annual drama of the Death and Revival of Spring or Summer in the many forms which it assumes, that the " counterfeit presentment " of spring or summer or the Vegetation Spirit is a *tree*, or part of a tree, or a puppet made of or adorned with leaves or boughs, or a human being similarly adorned.‡. The burning torches are likewise paralleled ; thus among the Slovenes the man who impersonates the Vegetation Spirit carries a lighted torch,§ while the carrying of lighted torches was part of the fertility-ritual of the Mysteries of Eleusis.‖ Again, the " hood " in the Axhey custom recalls the

---

* Dyer, work cited, pp. 30, seqq. and authorities there cited.
† Hone, " Table Book," 36.
‡ For examples, cf. " G.B.," chaps. x and xxviii, *passim*.
§ *Ibid.*, 128.
‖ For the Eleusinian ritual see Smith's " Dictionary of Classical Antiquities," s.v. " Eleusinia."

The earliest record of
a transaction involv—
ing a silver ball.
Entries in the famous
ST. COLUMB GREEN
BOOK in 1594 and 1595.

practice of decking an artificial puppet in human clothing, another common feature in spring customs.* Finally, the carrying of the holly-tree round the village at Brough, before the contest, clearly connects itself with the almost universal practice of taking the object or creature which in the spring festival is considered as the embodiment of the Spirit of Vegetation round the village in solemn procession.†

The irresistible conclusion is that the Brough tree-custom is a survival, not very much altered, of a rite in which a tree was employed and supposed to embody the Vegetation Spirit, and that the Axhey custom is of a similar nature but keeping less to the original form; it might be said that the former still remains ritual while the latter has passed from ritual into a game. It may be objected that the middle of January is too early for a rite in which the desired end is the revival of nature in spring (having regard to the usual times of spring festivals in general). But I do not think that this objection is justified. There is no special reason why such a rite should not be celebrated at any time after the winter solstice. We have already seen that the "Funeral of Kostroma" which purports to represent the *death* of summer is celebrated only a few days after the summer solstice. Further, in the case of the Axhey custom, this is intimately associated with another ritual survival held on the following day, the main feature in which was a procession of men dressed up to represent oxen.‡ This clearly has reference to the first agricultural labours of the year—the ploughing in preparation for the spring sowing—and it would not be unnatural in an agricultural community

---

* Cf. " G.B.," pp. 125-7, 307-14 for examples.
† *Ibid.*
‡ Dyer, work cited, 32. This is of course the same rite as that celebrated elsewhere in England, unassociated with any ball-game, on Plough Monday (first Monday after Twelfth Day). Cf. Frazer, " Spirits of the Corn and of the Wild (" G.B., " 3rd ed.), Vol. II, chap. xvii, *passim.*

for a vegetation rite to become associated with a ploughing rite. This seems to be the case at Axhey.

But why the fight over the tree? We have seen that in the " funeral of Kostroma " summer and winter fight for possession of the " corpse." Further, in the Mayday games in the Isle of Man, previously referred to, the two parties were each headed by a " Queen " and it was the prime object of the party of Winter to take the Queen of May prisoner.* We may conjecture that, if the tree in the original form of the Brough rite represented the Spirit of Vegetation, spring, or summer, then its capture by one party or the other may have been regarded, according to the principles of sympathetic magic, as influencing the revival of nature for good or evil, just as in the Eskimo rite alluded to the result is held to influence the severity of the winter. Again, it is possible that in the original rite the result was always predetermined, so that the party of summer was always victorious ; the fact that this is the usual arrangement in the " Battle of Summer and Winter " makes this indeed very probable. But we may go even further. In many parts of Europe in March or April is or was held a ceremony called " Carrying out Death." It bears a close resemblance to " Killing the Carnival " and is of the same nature. " Death " in this instance is a straw effigy, usually dressed in female attire ; and in Frazer's words it is " an embodiment of the tree-spirit or spirit of vegetation."† Now in many places, and particularly in Silesia, this effigy ends its career by being torn in pieces by the villagers, each one striving for a bit of it ; and the successful combatants bury their prizes in the fields " to make the corn grow " or put them in the mangers to cause the cattle to increase and multiply exceedingly. In some places it is believed that if those who have carried the effigy beat the cattle

---

* Train, loc. cit.
† " G.B.," 307-11, 314, 316.

with their sticks the beasts would grow specially fat and
bear many calves. At Leipzig in Germany the " Death "
was carried about and shown to all the young married
women to make them prolific.* This carrying about of
the effigy is not confined to the rite of " Carrying about
Death " ; we have seen it in " Killing the Carnival " and
in fact it is almost universal in all those forms of the spring
festival in which the spirit of spring or vegetation is considered as temporarily embodied in an effigy or in a human
or other animal ; this is done so that every member of the
community shall have opportunity to absorb, so to speak,
a portion of the fresh and vigorous life of which the effigy
or animal is, to borrow a term from physics, the conductor.
Now this feature of the procession is, as we have found,
one of the features of the Brough rite. Bearing all this
in mind, it seems reasonable to conclude that the customs
of Brough and Axhey represent the survivals of a ritual
act, celebrated at a time subject to local variation but
lying between the first lengthening of the days after the
winter solstice and the obvious commencement of summer
at the end of April or beginning of May, in which two
parties, representing summer or life and winter or death
contended in mimic combat over a tree or puppet considered as being the embodiment of the spirit of vegetation.
This rite is closely paralleled in the Mayday games in the
Isle of Man, where a human actor takes the place of the
puppet, and less closely in the " Funeral of Kostroma."
The powers of promoting fertility attributed to the represen-
tation of the vegetation spirit would cause its possession
to be a thing to be desired and a source of pride and
gratification.

We are now, I think, in a fair way towards the
solution of our problem. It will be remembered that
we set out to find instances of customs parallel to the

* *Ibid.*, 309, 314.

20

ball-games, but employing some other object in place of the ball. These we have found at Brough and Axhey. (We find, moreover, that the ritual procession surviving at Brough and so characteristic of spring festivals in general has its representative in at least one well-attested case among the ball-games—namely, that at Dorking, where the game was preceded by the carrying of the ball around the town by the players ; and it may not be altogether without significance that in this case the players were attired in fancy dress as the participants in a spring festival so frequently are.*) Lastly, we find in the high value assigned to the possession of the effigy, or a piece of it, in many spring festivals a parallel to the high value assigned to the possession of the ball in the ball-games.

From a consideration of the above evidence I am led to consider that the ball-games are derived from a rite like that of Brough (which in itself is a variant, seemingly peculiarly British, of the familiar " Battle of Summer and Winter ") by the substitution of the ball for the original tree or puppet. The explanation of this substitution is, I believe, most probably as follows. With the passage of time, belief in the inner significance of a ritual act dies unless it is always kept before the minds of the actors. In the case of countries coming under the influence of Christianity the officially hostile attitude of the Church to what it is pleased to term the " superstitions of the heathen " would hasten this death ; but the Church, though successful on the whole in destroying the old beliefs did not destroy the rites which the beliefs underlay. In fact, it did not as a rule essay this colossal task, save when a custom was unusually gross and repulsive or when it was too unmistakably pagan to be let alone. The more innocuous of the rites were let alone, or even pressed into the service of the new faith. So long after the old beliefs

---

* Letter to " Times " cited. Cf. " G.B."

were dead, the rites themselves were kept up—not infrequently from some vague feeling that their omission would bring bad luck ; or merely from reverence for the " mos majorum," the " tradition of the elders." But in all such cases they slowly degenerate with time and are ever subject to mutilation and loss, till their nature becomes thoroughly obscured. So I conjecture that the ball became substituted for the original tree or effigy simply because the real meaning of the rite had been lost in this way, it having degenerated into a mere game, kept up " for luck " or through the inertia of tradition. The popularity of the ball as a toy would then naturally lead to its substitution for the original object, just because the ball was so much better for the purpose than a clumsy lump of wood or bundle of straw. The substitution may well have given the derelict rite a new lease of life by completing its transformation into an exciting game played with a familiar and less uncouth object. Only at Brough, and to a less degree at Axhey, the rite in its purer form survives, through causes that we can do no more than conjecture. But there can hardly have failed to persist the feeling that there was " something " about the tree or bundle of straw or rags that made it different from ordinary every-day trees or bundles ; and this feeling would naturally be reflected into the ball, causing (reinforced no doubt by the simple emotion of gratification at success) its possession to be considered desirable and honourable.

The sole objection to this explanation which presents itself to me is as follows. We have seen that the ball-games are known in Brittany, and we have had reason to conclude that they were introduced into this district from Britain. Now so far as I have been able to discover the original form, which on the hypothesis here advanced was taken by the custom, is not known in Brittany. I have suggested that the acceptance of Christian beliefs may have

Hurling the Silver Ball at St Columb Major, Cornwall

had much to do with the loss of the real meaning of the rite and its consequent transformation into a popular game. It seems fairly certain that South Britain was nominally Christian by about 325 A.D., and the principal migrations to Armorica took place between 450 and 550 A.D. If it is maintained that the non-existence of the original rite in Brittany is evidence that the change to the ball-game had taken place before the immigrations from Britain, and that the change did not come about before the Christianization of the British, it may be objected that the time allowance for such a change is insufficient, bearing in mind the marked conservatism of people in a comparatively low stage of culture and the fact that the original rite has in fact survived till modern times in one or two places.

I believe that this objection, though plausible at first sight, is in reality too vague to be serious. In the first place we have no certain ground for the positive statement that the original rite was never known in Brittany. The mere fact that it does not apparently exist at present and that there is no record of its having existed is quite compatible with its having really had a home there, and then having died out before finding any literary or other record. Should it at any time be possible to show that this really was the case, the development into the ball-game may have come about either by independent evolution, or (more probably) by cultural drift from Britain at a subsequent date. In the second place, the suggestion put forward as to the part played by the influence of Christianity in the change, though very probable in itself, is a suggestion only, and must not be taken so strictly as to exclude the possibility of the rite having been in a decaying state before the Christianization of Britain. It must be remembered that countless beliefs and rituals acts have died of inanition, through the progress of culture, without the slightest assistance from Christianity. The religion of the Roman

Republic, for example, is full of instances of this. Thus the original rite *may* have lost its real meaning for its performers in Britain generations before the acceptance of the new faith.

Finally, the time allowance of over a century and a half, even if not considered sufficient for a general change, is not too small for a local one. If such a local change took place in south-western Britain at some time between the Christianization of this district and the migrations to Armorica, the ball-game may have been taken to the latter district in its modern form, and the change have later communicated itself to other parts of Britain.

Thus the objection may be countered in any of these three ways, all of which represent possibilities (although the second suggestion is advanced with more diffidence, since it is not easy to see why the belief in the significance of the rite should lapse before Christian times in a people of the low culture of the Britons). Personally I incline to the view that the third suggestion made is of a high degree of possibility. But in any case, seeing that these explanations may be set against the objection, which itself is admittedly not based on any positive fact (for we have no positive evidence whatever of the date of the first appearance of the ball-games, whatever their origin, and can only give a hypothetical date), it is clear that the latter is of too nebulous a nature to be of special importance.

I conclude, then, that the ball-games which we have examined, including the hurling game, are the degenerate and obscurely recognizable survivals of a ritual act which consisted in the combat of actors representing summer and winter for the possession of an object regarded as the embodiment of the spirit of vegetation—that is to say, they are the survivals of a rite of imitative magic intended to secure the rebirth of nature in spring.

ADDENDUM NOTE.

With reference to the late date of the hurling match at Helston, on the view of the custom's origin here put forward it is possible that its observance may have been post-dated to synchronise roughly with the important spring festival of the " Furry."